The
SOCKKIDS™
Meet Lincoln

The SockKids
PO Box 1130
East Northport, New York

ISBN 978-0-9727077-7-0 (0-9727077-7-8)
LCCN 2013914537

The SOCKKIDS™
Meet Lincoln

by Michael John Sullivan
and Susan Petrone

The sock drawer shook from side to side, which could only mean one thing: the Sockkids were dancing! It was Saturday in their human's house. What's so special about Saturday? Why, it's wash day! What sock doesn't like to take a swim in the washing machine?

"Whew, it sure is smelly in here," said Grandpa Bleach. "These kids may need the extra wash cycle."

"I need a long wash," said Stretch, a tube sock who spent most of his time with the humans playing sports.

His little sister, Rinse, took a sniff in his direction. "Yuck!" she said.

Rinse was very happy. She *loved* swimming in the washer. She adjusted her goggles and pretended to be a dolphin swimming up and down in the water. "Yay!" she squealed.

"Don't get fuzzies!" Rainbow said to her husband Parch, who loved to lounge in the dryer all day. "That includes you, too, Grandpa. No dozing."

The Sockkids laughed. Grandpa would often fall asleep in the dryer and wake up covered with fuzzies. Yes, fuzzies!

Fuzzies were those little knots that clung to their bodies. Then the humans would have to pull them off. The pinging pain sent even the most courageous sock to the nearest laundry basket for another wash. Oh, it was terrible to even *say* the word "fuzzies!"

One of the humans scooped up the entire Socker family and headed for the laundry room, where the water was already pouring into the washer. "Woo hoo!" shouted Stretch as he dove in. The warm, soapy water felt great and loosened his wool.

"Don't swim too far, Stretch," warned Grandpa Bleach. "Do you know what happens when socks go too far in the washing machine?"

"I know," Stretch said, looking away. "They get lost."

"I remember the first time I had my first wash. It was a mixed cycle with these awful bright colored shirts and smelly underwear falling all over me, and I was so scared when . . ."

Whoosh! Whoosh! The sound of the washer drowned out Grandpa Bleach's story. Stretch laughed as Grandpa's words floated up in a bubble. "Great story, Grandpa!" Stretch shouted. He jumped and tried to catch the bubble just as the spin cycle started. Whizzzzz! Around and around Stretch went!

Most of the time, socks just go into the washing machine with the rest of the clothes, get washed and dried, and put back in their drawer. But washing machines can be a special place for socks. During the spin cycle, socks can sometimes slip through time and go to another time and place in the world. People think the socks are lost but they've just gone visiting.

Poor Stretch. He was about to take a trip. "Help!" he cried, plunging back into the bath.

Too late!

Stretch whirled around so fast his eyes popped. He shut them tightly and felt himself falling. "Helppppp!" he pleaded.

He opened his eyes and found himself on a strange, hairy human leg. He looked up and saw a man with a beard wearing a tall black hat speaking to many people. Their feet were covered with muddy boots and torn socks.

"Four score and seven years ago, our fathers brought forth upon this continent a new nation, conceived in liberty, and dedicated to the proposition that all men are created equal," the man's voice boomed.

"Where did you come from?" the black sock on the tall man's other leg asked in surprise. "You're different from me. Are you a loose sock? What happened to your color? Do you have a soap issue?"

"I'm not a loose sock! I always look this way," Stretch said. "I'm just like you. A sock. I got lost in the washing machine."

"What is a washing machine?" the black sock asked.

"It's where we go to get clean."

The black sock stared at Stretch. "You can explain it to me another day. But you'll be safe on the feet of Abraham Lincoln. He is a special human. He treats all socks the same, no matter what they look like."

"Why is he special?" Stretch asked.

Stretch's new friend smiled. "He is the president of the United States, the most important human in the world and he cares about us. We are lucky to warm his feet this day."

"Even someone like me?" Stretch asked. "I am not from here."

"Yes," the black sock said.

Abraham Lincoln finished his speech. ". . . that this nation, under God, shall have a new birth of freedom— and that government of the people, by the people, for the people, shall not perish from the earth."

There was a long applause. "Where are we?" Stretch asked.

"Gettysburg, Pennsylvania."

Stretch gave a worried look. "What year is it?" he asked.

"1863."

"Oh, no! I've traveled really far!"

"Don't be afraid. My name is Meade."

"I'm Stretch."

"Well, Stretch, you will enjoy warming President Lincoln's feet. He never sleeps these days. He walks around and around his office some nights. Some nights I get dizzy!"

Meade grinned. "We are also washed with the best soap in the land. We are the best smelling socks in the United States."

"But I want to go back to my family," Stretch said.

"I will try and help you," promised Meade.

They rested as Lincoln rode in a carriage. The smell of the horses pulling them bothered Stretch, but Meade was used to it. He snoozed the whole way.

It was many hours later when the carriage stopped. Lincoln walked into a big white house. A woman greeted him. Lincoln called her "Mary," and they talked as they walked upstairs. It was the biggest, most beautiful house Stretch had ever seen.

After walking down several long hallways, Lincoln entered a large bedroom and sat down on the bed. He laughed as he took off his socks. "Mary, look at this!" He pointed to Stretch, holding him high up in the air.

"Oh my goodness!" Mary laughed. "I don't remember buying that white sock."

Stretch smiled and giggled.

"I have no idea where it came from," the President said. "How wonderful that I would wear one white and one black sock today."

They hugged. Stretch curled up into a ball and rolled against Lincoln. "I'm here for you, Mr. President," he whispered. "I will serve and keep your feet warm on the coldest of nights! I will protect you."

President Lincoln handed the socks to another human.
"It's wash time!" said Meade with excitement.

The human dropped them in a tub of hot water and soap. Meade floated with a big smile. Stretch clung onto the far side, afraid.

The human took Meade out and placed him on a wooden board. She took a wide stick and rolled it over him until all the water had dripped out of him.

The human came back to the tub and twirled the water around again, looking for Stretch. Around and around Stretch went. He felt dizzy. His eyes popped. He blinked several times and once again felt himself falling. "Oh no, not again!" he said. "Helpppppppp!" The word went up in a bubble as Stretch squeezed his eyes shut.

"Stretch, are you all right?" a voice asked.

"Mom?"

"Yes," Rainbow said. "You got lost, sweetie. What happened?"

"I saw President Lincoln!"

"Oh my goodness," Rainbow said with a big smile. "That was a big trip."

Stretch jumped high. "I met another sock named Meade. He was one of the bravest socks I ever met. He was happy to serve the president."

"I bet you were brave, too," his mother said.

Stretch smiled. "It's easy to be brave when you warm the feet of President Lincoln."

The End

The Authors

Michael John Sullivan is the creator of the SockKids. Constantly searching for his socks, he wondered whether the missing foot comforters had found another pair of feet to warm.

Before his interest in socks, Sullivan started writing his first novel while homeless, riding a NYC subway train at night. After being rescued off the train, he spent much of the past two decades raising two daughters while working at home.

Sullivan returned to his subway notes in 2007 and began writing *Necessary Heartbreak* (Simon & Schuster, Gallery Books imprint). *Library Journal* named *Necessary Heartbreak* one of the year's best for 2010.

His second novel, *Everybody's Daughter* (Fiction Studio Books, 2012) was named one of the best books of 2012 by TheExaminer.com. Sullivan has written articles about the plight of homelessness for CNN.com, *The Washington Post.com*, Beliefnet.com, the Huffington Post, and America Online's Patch.com service.

Susan Petrone's short fiction has been published by *Glimmer Train*, Featherproof Books, *The Cleveland Review*, *Muse*, *Conclave*, and *Whiskey Island*. Her first novel, *A Body at Rest*, was published in 2009 (Drinian Press). Her short story, "Monster Jones Wants to Creep You Out" (Conclave,2010) was nominated for a 2011 Pushcart Prize. She also writes about her beloved Cleveland Indians at ItsPronouncedLajaway. com for ESPN.com's SweetSpot network. In addition, she is a regular contributor to Cool Cleveland.com.

For more information on The SockKids, go to TheSockKids.com.

Recommended Viewing for Parents interested in learning more about President Lincoln

The highly acclaimed film—*Saving Lincoln*

Based on the true story of Abraham Lincoln (Tom Amandes) and his close friend, Ward Hill Lamon (Lea Coco), *Saving Lincoln* combines elements of theater and cinema to create a new visual world within vintage Civil War photographs. When the first assassination attempt occurs on the way to Washington in 1861, banjo-playing, pistol-wielding Lamon appoints himself Lincoln's bodyguard. From this unique perspective, Lamon witnesses every aspect of Lincoln's fiery trial as Commander-in-Chief, soothes his friend's tormented soul, and saves him from repeated attempts on his life. Lamon is away on a mission when Lincoln is killed, yet it is Lamon who redefines that tragic event in a surprising and uplifting manner. *Saving Lincoln* has been called "a new and different kind of cinematic experience . . . truly fascinating" (*Film Journal International*), as well as "brave, incisive, brilliant and entirely factual" (Harold Holzer, Lincoln author and authority).

Buy on Amazon: http://www.amazon.com/Saving-Lincoln
-Tom-Amandes/dp/B00D4CH1QM/ref=pd_rhf_gw_p_t_1_XT64

On Facebook: https://www.facebook.com/SavingLincoln

For more information about the film: SavingLincoln.com

Recommended Reading for Children and Parents:
Pippy's Wish By Maddie Ryan

Angel-in-Training Pippy is quirky, mischievous, lovable and enchanting. She can't wait to graduate, earn her wings and become a cool teen Angel.

Although she sometimes makes mistakes, her ingenuity and humor usually gets her out of trouble.

Except this time, it's gotten her INTO trouble.

Big trouble.

Can Pippy solve this one on her own?

Pippy's Wish is a fun, inspirational read for all ages.

Buy on Amazon: http://www.amazon.com/Pippys-Wish-ebook/dp/B00B0IMH20/ref=pd_sim_kstore_3

On Facebook: https://www.facebook.com/maddieryanchildrensauthor

On Twitter: https://twitter.com/MaddieRyan11

Made in the USA
Charleston, SC
27 September 2016